Make it Change!

Written by:
Anna Claybourne

Illustrated by:
Kimberley Scott and Venetia Dean

Published in paperback in 2014 by Wayland
Copyright © Wayland 2014

Wayland
338 Euston Road
London NW1 3BH

Wayland Australia
Hachette Children's Books
Level 17/207
Kent Street
Sydney, NSW 2000

Senior Editor: Julia Adams
Editor: Annabel Stones
Designer: Anthony Hannant (LittleRedAnt)
Illustrator (step-by-steps): Kimberley Scott
Illustrator (incidentals and final crafts): Venetia Dean
Proofreader & Indexer: Sara Harper

Dewey categorisation: 530.4

ISBN 978 0 7502 8384 7

Printed in China

1 3 5 7 9 10 8 6 4 2

Wayland is a division of Hachette Children's Books,
an Hachette UK company.
www.hachette.co.uk

Picture acknowledgements:
All photographs: Shutterstock

Contents

Change!

Change is happening all the time, all around us. Leaves turn brown in the autumn, puddles dry up and disappear in the sun, and clouds turn into rain, which falls on your head. You cook an egg, and it turns hard. You cook some butter, and it melts! Old cars get covered in rust, and old people's hair turns white. But why do things change?

POP!
BUBBLE
BUBBLE

SIZZLE

WHAT MAKES THINGS CHANGE?

All the things around us are made of tiny parts called atoms, and molecules – which are made of atoms joined together. When things warm up, cool down, or are mixed together, this can make the atoms and molecules behave differently.

MMM, SMELLS FRESH!

Washing is wet when you hang it up, then it changes and becomes dry in the breeze and sunshine.

TURN UP THE HEAT

Heating things up makes atoms and molecules move faster and separate from each other, which can make a solid like chocolate melt into a liquid.

MAKING MIXTURES

When some substances are mixed together, it causes a chemical reaction, which can make one substance change into another.

YUM, YUM!

BEING A SCIENTIST

In this book there are lots of easy experiments that let you explore amazing, surprising and exciting changes. But don't forget to keep your scientist's hat on!

• Follow the instructions and watch what happens carefully.

• Do experiments more than once if you can, to check they always work the same way.

• Keep a record of your results by writing them down, drawing pictures or taking photos of them.

5

Turn a penny green

Copper coins normally look a dull brown colour. Try making them change colour using a chemical reaction.

Here's What to Do...

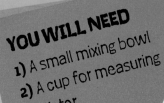

YOU WILL NEED
1) A small mixing bowl
2) A cup for measuring
3) Water
4) White vinegar
5) Table salt
6) A teaspoon
7) Old, well-used copper coins
8) Kitchen paper

1. Half-fill the bowl with water and stir in half a cup of white vinegar and a teaspoon of salt.

2. Take a copper coin and hold it halfway into the water for 20 seconds. What happens?

3. Now drop some more coins into the water and leave them there for 5 minutes.

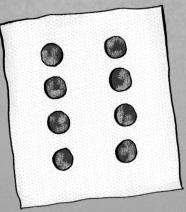

4. Carefully take them out and lay them on some kitchen paper for an hour. What happens?

WHAT'S GOING ON?

Coins become dull because they react with the air and get a coating on them. When you dip a coin into your mixture, the acid in the vinegar dissolves the coating, making the coins shiny.

However, if you leave the coins covered with the salt and acid, it helps them to react more quickly with the air, creating a green coating (called malachite) that's made of copper and oxygen, a gas found in the air.

The Statue of Liberty is made of copper and was shiny brown to start with. She has now turned green due to chemical reactions.

! TROUBLESHOOTER

Don't dry or wipe the coins when you take them out – leave them wet on top.

WHAT IS A CHEMICAL REACTION?

A chemical reaction happens when substances mix together. But not all mixtures cause a reaction. It only happens if the molecules can easily rearrange themselves to make new molecules.

Cu

Cu + O O → Cu O

Cu O

Cu

WHAT NEXT?

Vinegar is a type of chemical called an acid. Some other household substances are acids too, like lemon juice and fizzy drinks (cola or lemonade). See if the experiment works if you use them instead of vinegar.

Lava volcano

Use this exciting chemical reaction to make a model volcano erupt.

YOU WILL NEED
1) Modelling clay
2) A large tray
3) Bicarbonate of soda, also called baking soda
4) White vinegar
5) Red or orange food colouring
6) A teaspoon
7) A small jug

Here's What to Do...

1. Model a small volcano, about 10–15 cm high, out of modelling clay, making a deep hole in the middle with your finger.

2. Stand the volcano on the tray to catch the messy eruption.

3. Drop a teaspoonful of bicarbonate of soda into the hole in the volcano, along with a few drops of food colouring to make a lava colour.

4. Put a few teaspoons of white vinegar into the jug, then pour it carefully into the hole.

WHAT'S GOING ON?

When the acid vinegar meets the bicarbonate of soda, there's a strong, sudden chemical reaction. The ingredients change, making different, new substances instead. One of these is a gas called carbon dioxide. The bubbles of gas turn the mixture into a frothy foam that expands (gets bigger) and bursts out of the volcano like lava.

! TROUBLESHOOTER

Make sure the hole isn't too filled up with the bicarbonate of soda – leave plenty of space for vinegar.

TASTY BUBBLES

Carbon dioxide is often found in food – it's what makes the bubbles in bread and fizzy drinks.

WHAT NEXT?

Try mixing a little bicarbonate of soda and vinegar inside a sealable food bag, then quickly seal it shut. Do this outside and stand well back! The expanding gas will pop the bag open.

The red cabbage test

Use red cabbage to create colour-changing chemical reactions.

YOU WILL NEED

1) A fresh red cabbage
2) A grater
3) A mixing bowl
4) Water
5) A rolling pin
6) A sieve
7) 6 paper or plastic cups

Here's What to Do...

1. Grate a few tablespoons of red cabbage into the bowl and add enough water to cover it.

2. Mash or crush the cabbage with the rolling pin until the water turns purple.

3. Sieve the mixture to get out the cabbage lumps, and keep the liquid.

4. Pour a little of the liquid into each of your cups.

5. Now test different substances by dropping a little of them into a cup, and looking at what happens.

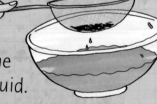

Toothpaste

Washing-up liquid

IO

SUBSTANCES TO TRY:

Vinegar
Lemon juice
Bicarbonate of soda
Toothpaste
Fizzy drinks
Washing-up liquid

WHAT'S GOING ON?

This experiment is a way of finding out if a substance is an acid, or the opposite of an acid, an alkali. When an acid mixes with the red cabbage liquid, it reacts and changes colour, becoming more red. Alkalis make the liquid more blue. This kind of test is called a litmus test.

TROUBLESHOOTER

Use cups that are clear or plain white, so you can see the colour of the liquid clearly.

OUCH!

Bee and ant stings contain a type of acid, while wasp stings contain an alkali. Both types of chemical are painful when they get under your skin!

WHAT NEXT?

What else can you think of to test? Can you change the colour of the liquid using one substance, then change it back again using another?

Exploding drinks

This explosion isn't actually a chemical reaction, though it looks like one. You need to do this outdoors!

YOU WILL NEED
1) A bottle of diet fizzy drink
2) Sweets with a rough, non-shiny surface (mints work well!)
3) Outdoor space

Here's What to Do...

1. Open the bottle of fizzy drink and stand it on the ground.

2. Drop a few sweets into the top.

3. Quickly stand back!

Fizzy Pop!

WHAT'S GOING ON?

The drink froths and foams, or even shoots out of the bottle, because of the carbon dioxide gas it contains. Normally, when you open a fizzy drink, the gas bubbles come out slowly. But the rough surface of the sweets helps the gas to separate from the water, and form big bubbles very fast. They can't all fit in the bottle, so the foamy liquid splurges out.

TROUBLESHOOTER

If you can't get a diet drink, a normal fizzy drink will also work, though the sugar may slow down the effect slightly.

DISSOLVING

When a fizzy drink is in its bottle with the lid on, the carbon dioxide gas is dissolved in it. This means it is broken into tiny bits and mixed into the drink. Solids can be dissolved too. For example if you stir sugar into tea, it dissolves. You can't see it, but it's still there.

WHAT NEXT?

What happens if you crush or break up the sweets first? Does it work better?

Does the experiment work if you put in other things, like a spoonful of salt, sugar or sand?

Make salt disappear and reappear

Salt dissolves easily in water, becoming invisible. You can make it reappear by making a crystal.

YOU WILL NEED

1) A pan
2) Water
3) Table salt
4) A heatproof jug
5) A saucer
6) A pencil
7) String

Here's What to Do...

1. Ask an adult to heat the pan of water and stir in and dissolve as much salt as possible.

2. They should let the water cool, then carefully pour the salty water into the jug, leaving any undissolved salt in the pan.

You can't see the salt, but you can taste a tiny bit of the water to check it's there.

3. Pour a little salty water onto the saucer, and leave it somewhere warm. The water will slowly dry up, leaving little square salt crystals.

4. Tie a piece of string to a pencil, wet the string and roll it in the salt crystals. Balance the pencil across the jug with the string dangling into the water, and leave it somewhere safe.

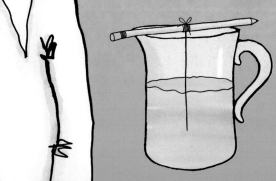

WHAT'S GOING ON?

When salt is stirred into hot water, it dissolves. But the salt is still there, waiting to form back into crystals. When the water dries up, or evaporates, bits of salt are left behind. When you put salt crystals on the string in the salty water, more and more salt sticks to them, growing a bigger and bigger crystal.

Salty water is all around us – in the sea, in foods such as cans of tuna and sweetcorn, even in our blood and body organs where it's essential for life.

WHAT NEXT?

Precious stones are crystals too. Crystals form and grow in regular shapes, like cubes or hexagons.

Can you find any other crystals in your home?

Rubbery bones

Bones are hard and stiff – that's how they hold us up. So how can you change a hard bone into a rubbery, bendy one?

YOU WILL NEED

1) A chicken leg bone, saved from a roast chicken or drumstick
2) White vinegar
3) A food container with a lid
4) Kitchen paper

1. Pick all the meat off the chicken bone and wash it carefully. Can you bend it at all?

2. Put the bone in the food container with enough white vinegar to cover it, and put the lid on.

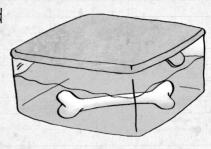

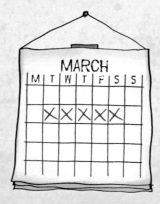

3. Leave it in a safe place for 5 days.

4. Take it out, rinse it in water, and dry it on kitchen paper. Now try to bend it.

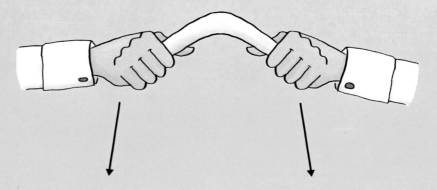

WHAT'S GOING ON?

The reason bones are hard is because they contain hard minerals – especially a substance called calcium, which is also found in many types of rock. Vinegar, a type of acid, is very good at dissolving calcium. As the vinegar soaks into the chicken bone, it dissolves the calcium, leaving a softer substance, known as collagen.

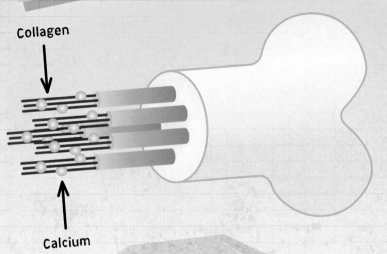

Collagen

Calcium

TROUBLESHOOTER

You can use dark-coloured vinegar if that's all you have – it's just a bit messier.

BENDY BONES

Part of your skeleton, including the tip of your nose and the joints in your back, are made of a bendy substance called cartilage, instead of bone. This helps some parts of our bodies to be more flexible. A shark's skeleton is all made of cartilage, to help it twist and bend in the water.

WHAT NEXT?

Can you actually tie your chicken bone in a knot?

Are any parts of your skeleton bendy and not hard? Try wiggling the tip of your nose.

Bottle balloon

Things also change when they heat up and cool down. One thing they do is get bigger and smaller.

Here's What to Do...

YOU WILL NEED

1) A balloon
2) A medium-sized, empty plastic drinks bottle
3) A cold fridge
4) A warm radiator or sunny windowsill

1. Stretch the opening of the uninflated balloon over the neck of the bottle.

2. Put the bottle and balloon in the fridge for a few minutes. What happens?

3. Take them out and stand the bottle somewhere warm, like on top of a radiator or on a sunny windowsill. What happens?

WHAT'S GOING ON?

Air is made up of gases. The gases are made of tiny molecules zooming around and crashing into each other. When a gas warms up, its molecules move faster and hit each other harder. This makes them spread out more and expand, taking up more space, and expanding the balloon. When air cools down, the molecules get slower and closer together, and the gas contracts, or shrinks.

In warm air, the molecules are further apart, so the air is lighter than cold air. This is why hot air balloons and paper fire lanterns float.

Most solids and liquids also get bigger as they get warmer, and smaller as they get cooler.

Radiator heats air

TROUBLESHOOTER

If the fridge doesn't make a big difference, try the freezer, or stand the bottle in a bowl of ice.

WHAT NEXT?

Try this experiment with a glass bottle. Wet the opening of the bottle with water and put a wet coin over the top. Hold the bottle in warm hands, or stand it on a radiator, to warm up the air inside. The expanding air will push the coin and make it jump.

19

Magic ice cubes

This experiment also works as a magic trick! Challenge your friends to pick up an ice cube with a piece of string and some salt, without touching it.

YOU WILL NEED
1) Several ice cubes
2) A bowl
3) Water
4) String
5) Table salt

Here's What to Do...

1. Fill the bowl with water and put in a few ice cubes. Can your friends get them out using the string? It's tricky!

2. To do it, dip the string in the water then lie it across the tops of the ice cubes.

3. Then sprinkle salt all over the ice cubes, and wait 30-60 seconds.

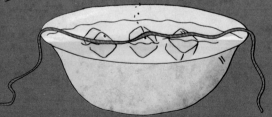

4. Now lift one end of the string. It should be stuck to the ice cubes and will pick them up.

WHAT'S GOING ON?

Water freezes into ice at freezing temperature, 0°Celsius. However, salty water freezes at a lower temperature. When salt touches the ice cubes, it makes a layer of salty water which is not cold enough to freeze, so the surface of the ice cube melts a little, and the string soaks into it. Then, the salt gradually flows away and the ice cubes freeze at 0°C again, holding the string beneath ice.

! TROUBLESHOOTER

Rough parcel string works well – avoid very smooth string.

STRANGE WATER

Usually, substances always shrink as they get colder. But when water freezes into ice, its molecules push apart, and it actually expands a little. This means ice is less dense (heavy for its size) than water, and floats.

WHAT NEXT?

Does it work with a toothpick or lolly stick?

Can you work out why putting salt on icy roads makes them safer?

Plastic bag ice cream

You can make ice cream in a few minutes with ice, salt and a bit of shaking!

YOU WILL NEED

1) Full-fat milk
2) Sugar
3) Vanilla essence
4) Sealable sandwich bags
5) A larger plastic shopping bag or food bag
6) A large bag or several trays of ice cubes
7) A large packet of table salt or rock salt

SUGAR

1. Put 250 ml (one cup) of milk, 4 teaspoons of sugar and a few drops of vanilla essence into a sandwich bag and seal it shut.

2. Put this bag inside a second sandwich bag and seal it shut, to protect against leaks.

3. Fill the larger bag with ice cubes, and mix in a large handful of salt.

4. Tuck the bag of milk into the middle of the ice and salt mixture, hold it closed, and shake the whole bag for 5 minutes. Then take out your ice cream!

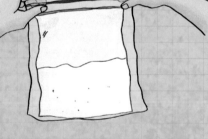

WHAT'S GOING ON?

The salt lowers the freezing temperature of the ice, making it start to melt. Melting takes energy, which sucks heat out of the bag of milk, and it freezes into ice cream.

! TROUBLESHOOTER

Rock salt for de-icing pavements is best of all, if you have any, but other salt works too. Wipe the ice cream bag when you get it out to make sure no salt gets in.

QUICK SHAKE!

To make smooth, creamy ice cream, you have to freeze it fast and keep it moving. You do this by shaking, mixing or churning it in a machine. This helps to mix in a little air and keep the ice crystals small, so it isn't too hard and crunchy.

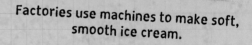

Factories use machines to make soft, smooth ice cream.

WHAT NEXT?

Once you can make ice cream, try different flavours instead of vanilla. See if it works with mint essence, banana milk powder or choc chips!

23

Pure water still

A still is a way to separate water from things that are mixed into it, such as dissolved salt.

YOU WILL NEED

1) Warm tap water
2) Table salt
3) A heatproof bowl
4) A small glass
5) Clingfilm or plastic food wrap
6) Sticky tape
7) A coin

Here's What to Do...

1. Half-fill the bowl with warm water and stir in several tablespoonfuls of salt until it dissolves. Taste a tiny bit of the water to check it is salty.

SALT

2. Stand the empty glass or jug in the bowl – it should be lower than the edge of the bowl, but taller than the water level.

3. Spread a piece of clingfilm or food wrap tightly over the bowl. Tape it in place if it won't stick.

4. Put the coin in the middle of the clingfilm, right over the empty glass.

5. Now carefully put the still somewhere warm, like on a windowsill in bright sunshine.

WHAT'S GOING ON?

After a while, you should end up with some clear water in the glass. Taste it to see if the salt is gone. Heat makes the water start to evaporate – change into a gas (called water vapour) – leaving the salt behind. The water vapour gets trapped under the plastic film, where it condenses – turns back into a liquid. Because the coin is weighing the plastic down in the middle, the water droplets run down the underside of the plastic film and drip into the glass.

! TROUBLESHOOTER

If it's not sunny, it should still work in a warm room, just a bit more slowly.

In hot jungles, the air is damp because water vapour evaporates from the leaves of plants.

CHANGING TO A GAS

Water changes into water vapour at boiling temperature, 100°C. But it also evaporates slowly at lower temperatures. That's why puddles dry in the sun and washing dries on a line.

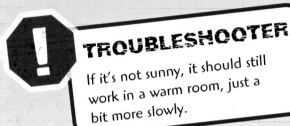

WHAT NEXT?

Try the experiment with water with food colouring in it, or with milk or squash. Does it work?

Make your own butter

Butter is made from cream – but how does liquid cream change into solid butter? You need to shake it.

Here's What to Do...

1. Make sure your jar or container is completely clean and dry.

2. Half-fill it with cream and put the lid on tightly.

CREAM

3. Now shake it – up and down, to and fro, and round and round. Take turns with friends or family if your arms get tired!

4. After around 10 minutes of shaking you should hear a slapping sound. This means the cream has changed into butter and watery buttermilk.

5. Pour away the buttermilk and rinse your butter in cold water a few times, then dry it in kitchen paper. It's ready to spread on a cracker and eat!

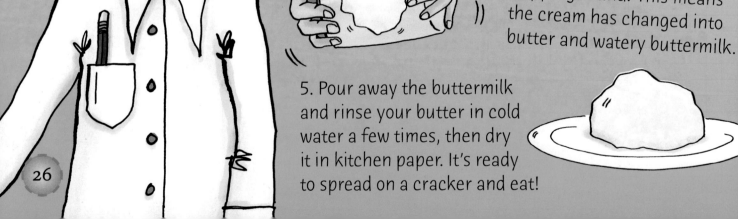

WHAT'S GOING ON?

Cream is a type of substance called an emulsion. It's made of watery liquid with tiny droplets of fat in it. Shaking makes the fat droplets bump and stick together. The more you shake, the more they stick until you have a big lump of fat (the butter) separated from the liquid (buttermilk).

TROUBLESHOOTER

It works best if the cream is room temperature, so leave it out of the fridge for a bit first if possible.

BUTTER CHURNS

Most butter is made in factories, by spinning cream around in a churning machine, which looks like a giant washing machine. Before machines, people used butter churns, wooden barrels which they had to turn or shake by hand.

WHAT NEXT?

Does it work with other types of cream, or full-fat milk?

Can you use your butter to make something else, like a cake?

Mould garden

If you leave an apple in the fruit bowl or bread in the bread bin for too long, it will turn mouldy and change into something disgusting. But why?

YOU WILL NEED

1) A clear glass jar with a tight lid, that you don't mind throwing away
2) Water
3) Glue
4) Sticky tape
5) Leftover food: try fruit, vegetables, bread, cake and cheese

Here's What to Do...

1. Make sure your jar is clean inside and the lid fits tightly.

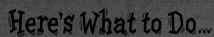

2. Wet a few pieces of food with water and put them into the jar, side by side.

DON'T use meat or fish – they will be too stinky and could contain dangerous germs.

3. Put glue around the top of the jar, put the lid on tightly and seal it with tape.

GLUE

4. Put the jar in a safe place and check it every day to see what happens.

DON'T open the jar! – it will let mould out. Throw it away after a few days.

WHAT'S GOING ON?

As the food goes mouldy, it may grow furry blobs or white or green patches, and start to collapse. Moulds are a type of fungi, living things related to mushrooms. They spread by releasing spores, like tiny seeds, into the air. These land on food and eventually start growing and feeding on it. Normally, we eat food or throw it away before mould can grow.

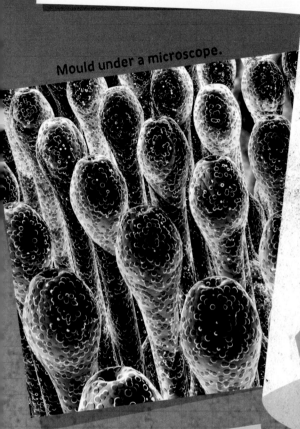

Mould under a microscope.

USEFUL MOULD

We use some types of mould to make medicines, and the 'veins' in blue cheese are also made of mould!

WHAT NEXT?

Can you take a photo of the jar at the same time every day to record what happens? You can put the photos together at the end to make a time-lapse sequence of the mould growing.

Glossary

acid A type of chemical.

alkali A type of chemical.

atoms Tiny units that substances are made of.

calcium A mineral found in bones and in some rocks.

carbon dioxide A type of gas.

cartilage A bendy material that makes up part of the skeleton.

Celsius A scale for measuring temperature.

condense To change from a gas into a liquid.

contract To get smaller.

copper A type of metal.

crystal A solid substance with a naturally regular shape.

dissolve To become mixed into a liquid and broken down into tiny parts.

emulsion A substance made of a liquid with droplets of another substance in it.

energy The power to do work or make things happen.

evaporate To change from a liquid into a gas.

expand To get bigger.

flexible Another word for bendy.

fungi A group of living things that includes moulds and mushrooms.

gas A substance in which molecules float around freely.

litmus test A test that uses colours to show whether a substance is acid or alkali.

mineral A naturally existing, pure, solid substance.

molecules Groups of atoms that make up substances.

oxygen A type of gas found in the air.

spores Tiny seed-like parts released by fungi.

water vapour Water in the form of a gas.

further reading

BOOKS:

Crazy Concoctions: A Mad Scientist's Guide to Messy Mixtures
by Jordan D. Brown, Imagine Publishing, 2012

Chemtastrophe! Kitchen Chemistry
by Jon Eben, Crabtree Publishing, 2011

Matter Matters! (Super Science)
by Tom Adams, Templar, 2012

WEBSITES

Zoom Science: Chemistry
pbskids.org/zoom/activities/
sci/#chemistry

BBC Bitesize: Material Science
http://www.bbc.co.uk/bitesize/ks2/
science/materials/

Index